THE ORIGIN
OF STOWE SCHOOL

Photograph by Elliott & Fry, London

EDWARD HENRY MONTAUBAN. M.A.
WHO FIRST IMAGINED A SCHOOL AT STOWE
AND BECAME A MEMBER OF ITS
ORIGINAL GOVERNING BODY

THE ORIGIN
OF
STOWE SCHOOL

BY

THE HON. SIR REGINALD P. CROOM-JOHNSON

W. S. COWELL LTD

IPSWICH AND LONDON

First published in 1953
Made and printed by W. S. Cowell Ltd
at their press in the Butter Market
Ipswich

I

A HANDSOME AND WELL-WRITTEN VOLUME[1] HAS RECORDED the remarkable growth and development physically and institutionally of Stowe School in the first thirty years of its life. Before it is too late, however, there should be related how the idea of a new public school germinated which resulted in the foundation of Stowe; and how it came about that the thought of a new great public school arose, and that at a time of national financial stringency.

Why was a new school thought to be necessary? Who first put forward the idea and whence came the inspiration? Who first imagined the great buildings being preserved, extended, and put to educational uses? What were the aims of the originators? Why at Stowe?

The story has not hitherto been written, nor has sufficient credit been given to the original pioneer. It is difficult to believe that little more than thirty years ago there was a danger, and even a likelihood, that the present mansion might be demolished, all its architectural and decorative beauties be torn down, its grounds and wonderful gardens laid out as building sites and covered with streets and houses. Today, restored, improved and enlarged, with its new chapel, extensive playing-fields, additional buildings, its memorial to the large number of old Stoics who gave their all, fighting in the Second World War, Stowe stands a monument of success and inspired determination and achievement.

This little work is intended as a brief account of how it all came about and as a tribute to the man who, appreciating the urgent necessity for more public schools, first envisaged, in 1921, a new school at Stowe – Edward Henry Montauban, M.A.

How came it that parents suddenly began to realize that the number of big public schools was insufficient; that without it they might not get their sons into a public school; that the demand for

[1] *Stowe: House and School*, by Alastair Macdonald. W. S. Cowell Ltd, 1951.

places largely exceeded the available vacancies? The answer is not simple.

The unexpectedly swift movement of events on the European battle-fronts in the late summer and autumn of 1918 which culminated in the armistice of 11 November of that year, brought to notice that during the war fathers had not realized the growth in age educationally of their sons. They knew, of course, that a state of war would not continue indefinitely; nevertheless, the armistice came as a shock and taught us that in our private family affairs we had not thought sufficiently during the war of the passage of time. We had not paid enough attention to the necessary arrangements for educating our sons, or considered what plans we ought to make for bringing them up, or educating them for careers on the basis of a world at peace. Thus it came about, when their future education had to be considered, that a sudden outbreak of peace found a large number of parents had omitted to reserve places for their sons at any public school. Faced with what appeared to them to be a sudden emergency, they discovered that there were few vacancies. They had not appreciated that when the time came to send a boy to a public school there would be any difficulty in getting him accepted, not merely at one of the best schools but at almost any school.

Some parents seemingly woke up suddenly to the necessity of preparing their sons by starting them on the education ladder for a new and harder world or for giving them a better chance than their fathers had had. Gone were the comfortable and expansive days of the Edwardian era; more parents began to take a much greater interest in education generally, its influence on careers, and became more vitally interested in types and degrees of education. It was not surprising, therefore, that the pressure on the best schools grew and grew. Small wonder that some fathers were surprised to find that their own old schools could not find room for their sons and that other schools had no vacancies to offer them. Directly after the armistice it speedily became apparent that the demand greatly exceeded the available vacancies; this progressively and rapidly became worse, and within a brief time the situation was acute. Even before the end of hostilities the number of parents asking for a public school education for their sons was increasing rapidly. Our population had increased considerably whilst the number of public schools had remained constant. Some parents wished to give their children what they considered was a better chance; some were induced by what can only be regarded as social and not educational reasons. Some people thought that this pressure would be only temporary, but events proved that that view was fallacious. The number of places reserved in the old grammar schools for pupils from the secondary schools, already, in the view of some of us, too high a proportion, was increased, and again the effect was to pre-judice the minds of some parents and make them prefer not to send their sons to those excellent old foundations.

II

THE RESERVATION OF A LARGE PROPORTION OF PLACES
under a so-called scholarship programme arranged by the Board
of Education under certain regulations for pupils from the elementary and secondary schools, had the effect of inducing some parents
to be dissatisfied on other than educational grounds with the daily
grammar schools or to make them wish to send their sons to schools
which they thought might provide something better. Some wanted
to send their sons away from home for various reasons; they turned
to the boarding house system and, desiring established schools of
tradition not in private ownership, they turned naturally at first to
the existing lesser public schools. The grammar schools were also
feeling the pressure for the vacancies not reserved for the Board
of Education nominees, so that even those fathers who were old
grammar school boys felt drawn by the public school tradition.
In addition, a number of entries were received or attempted from
parents settled in the Dominions or Colonies, from men who had
been attracted by the public school men they had met and fought
alongside during the hostilities. The natural increase of population
already mentioned had its influence too; and the wealth which had
poured into the country after the conclusion of the South African
war persuaded some parents to spend a larger portion of their
incomes on educating their children. Possibly the pressure had
existed before the war broke out in 1914 but, looking back to 1920,
at least there can be no question that the pressure of applicants for
entry at that time was far beyond the total capacity of most of the
existing schools in places, accommodation, and staff. Applications
for reservation of places for future terms became almost a night-
mare to house-masters and others. The then existing great public
schools had felt the pressure for years, but now the burden was being
felt by the lesser ones too. Eton, Harrow, and Winchester were
known to be full for many years to come. Rugby, Clifton, Wellington,

4

Marlborough, Haileybury, Sherborne, and many others, were over-whelmed with applications far in excess of possible acceptance, while the two schools offering a more definite 'modern' training were unlikely to have any but chance vacancies for years. Almost every school had a long waiting-list. It was easy to say that the crisis was an artificial one or that parents desiring to be on the safe side for the future entered their sons at several schools to ensure a vacancy when the appropriate time arrived, or entered them at birth or too soon. That easy answer did not meet the trouble.

Educationalists and others interested in education for boys between the ages of from $13\frac{1}{2}$ to $17\frac{1}{2}$ onwards found it impossible to find a solution for this growing and urgent problem. Enlarge-ment of the existing big schools was thought to be undesirable; many of them already contained too many pupils; to enlarge some of the smaller and more localized schools might adversely affect their local usefulness and traditions or destroy the purposes for which they were established. The grammar schools were mostly in large centres of population, difficult to extend or lacking land for suitable playing-fields, which would become necessary; the buildings were not to be easily enlarged except at extravagant cost, money was difficult to raise, and land for playing-fields was unobtainable.

No new big public schools for boys had been founded for some sixty years, and there were not wanting those who expressed the opinion that no one would want to send his son to a new school without that vague thing called tradition. Finally, the existing schools in the front rank were already big enough, if not too big, with more than a sufficiency of pupils and staff, teaching and other-wise, so that the idea of enlarging them was ruled out by the best expert opinion. In about 1920 there came the first of the post-war trade slumps; the added difficulties of raising finance apparently frightened a number of people from attempting to grapple with this seemingly insoluble problem. At all events, nobody did, or else only a few realized its size, gravity, or urgency.

III

LIGHT CAME AT FIRST FROM AN UNSUSPECTED QUARTER. A small number of schoolmasters had, in 1893, formed themselves into a body known at first as the Association of Preparatory Schools (later to be incorporated and recognized under the initials I.A.P.S.), its main object was 'to advance the interests of Education, especially as affecting Preparatory Schools'.

This Association proved of great value, and by 1920 comprised some six hundred members. Its affairs were directed by a Council at headquarters and locally by committees in twelve districts. E. H. Montauban, already a member of the main Council, acted also as secretary of the London branch; himself the proprietor of a highly prosperous preparatory school at Hampstead, and an educationalist of ability and vision. He, in the above offices, had access to the opinions of very many of his fellow-headmasters, and experienced with them the difficulty of getting places for all his pupils in the public schools. The problem was not really pressing for boys up to scholarship standard, for the clever boy, or the good examinee; the trouble was to find vacancies for the ordinary sound preparatory schoolboy on leaving – in fact, for just the type of boy that had most to gain from a public school education and whose parents were prepared to make every sacrifice to educate their sons. Parents pressed and complained and became anxious and worried.

Montauban, forced perhaps by this pressure, began to consider the possibility of finding a way out of this impasse, and the solution appeared to him to lie in the establishing of one or more new public schools. He began by bringing the idea before the members of his London branch. He was told that the I.A.P.S. had not been established to 'run' a public school, and all the manifest difficulties and problems were pointed out to him by less courageous people with restless reiteration, but he never lost hope or courage; by constant

6

effort he succeeded in interesting his branch in the idea, and ultimately he persuaded the Parent Body to put the subject on its agenda for discussion. By his own almost unaided efforts he interested the parents of a number of his pupils and of his fellow-schoolmasters in the question. He circularized his fellow-members and invited them to express their opinions on the need for a new school. It had to be made clear that a new school was not in any sense to be a competitor with the then existing ones. Those who were invited to support it were invited to run a risk. The existing great schools, it was pointed out, had nothing to fear from an addition to their number: what was wanted was more of them to fill up the manifest insufficiency. Subsidizing any of the existing smaller schools or increasing their buildings would not meet the problem. A new school, with the possibility of some modern developments — not unduly trammelled by old traditions or practices, would, it was thought, make an appeal to those who believed in what a modern public school should provide.

From the outset, however, Montauban insisted that what he had in mind was a new GREAT public school. The new schools established from the 1840's onwards started in quite a small way in buildings not specially built for the purpose, but from the outset Montauban insisted that what he was after was something which was ultimately to take a foremost place, and he aimed at its being among the first six. It was a bold project, needing much courage in the then state of our national trade and finances. Montauban conducted his own agitation among his professional friends and colleagues and among the parents of his large number of pupils.

At the annual general conference of the Association in December 1920 the Council were instructed to make investigations into a scheme which had been submitted by Montauban for providing the finance for a new school; they set up a small sub-committee of four, of which he was a member. The conference had decided to adopt Montauban's idea for further investigation, notwithstanding a certain amount of opposition based on various grounds, but opposition speedily yielded to the overwhelming arguments put

7

forward and the urgent necessity of the case. It had taken Montauban at least eighteen months of constant endeavour to reach that stage.

On 21 May 1921 a discussion on a proposal to found one or more new public schools was started in *The Times Educational Supplement*, and public interest began to widen.

IV

IT WAS IN THAT YEAR, 1921, THAT IT WAS ANNOUNCED
that for family reasons an auction sale was to be held at the historic
mansion of the family of the last of the Dukes of Buckingham and
Chandos at Stowe House, Buckingham. It was Montauban's
inspiration that first envisaged that the new public school such as he
was campaigning for should be established at Stowe. Before the
sale took place he took a party of friends likely to be interested to
view and investigate the house and grounds, to see if they thought
that Stowe would be a suitable place in which to establish a new
school. They picnicked in the great dining-room, with its dining-
table about the length of a cricket pitch, and, indeed, tested it
and came away fully impressed with all that they saw. The sale
of the furniture started on 4 July 1921, and lasted for nineteen
days, in some 4,000 lots in a catalogue of 230 pages and,
naturally, received a great deal of publicity. The manor house
(originally erected in 1560) had been rebuilt by the Duke at vast
cost in the eighteenth century. The noble mansion which had
taken its place was sold with some of the surrounding land for
£35,000, in one lot, to a Mr Shaw. There had been an earlier sale
of some of the furniture in 1848, and this time practically everything was disposed of. The famous grounds laid out by Kent, and
later by 'Capability' Brown, surrounding the mansions, were left
available; the great estate, with its farms, etc, was divided up and
sold, but many of the family and other monuments were left
standing.

In the next few months Montauban was not idle. He obtained
support for his idea from many quarters. Some hundreds of school-
masters, parents, and other persons interested in education promised
him general support. Meantime, with the help of the junior counsel
of the I.A.P.S., their solicitor, and other members, but in their
private capacity, Montauban had approached the purchaser of the

mansion itself. What to do with it was, indeed, a problem. No one could afford to inhabit it. It was described publicly by an opponent as a 'white elephant', but to pull it down, with all its beauty of decoration, design, and architectural feature, would have been an act of vandalism. The use of great houses as hospitals, public institutions, and the like, was reaching saturation point. In the end the purchaser expressed his willingness to hand over the mansion, but stripped of its internal carvings and decorations, with 280 acres, as a gift for the purpose of a new school, provided a suitable endowment or finance could be obtained.

By the end of October 1921 Montauban had already had prepared in print a financial scheme[1] under which preparatory schools were invited to make a gift of £50 to £150 towards the funds required to start a school in return for which they would each be able to nominate suitable boys for vacancies; they were to be boys of public school age, $13\frac{1}{2}$ to 14, coming from recognized preparatory schools, i.e. members of the I.A.P.S.

The heads of the Oxford and Cambridge Colleges were approached and the headmasters of preparatory schools (all by Montauban himself). A great many situations had been considered, but when it was announced that Stowe House was in the market and was likely to be either sold or demolished, it was Montauban who took parties of interested people to inspect the place. He even took and furnished a house at Buckingham in which to entertain interested persons, so as more conveniently to show them over the house and grounds and discuss ideas. The house and its surroundings made its own appeal, and those who were interested in the idea of a new great school very quickly gave up any thought of its being established anywhere else; thereafter all the publicity referred to a new school at Stowe. One individual, as we have said, referred to the house as a 'white elephant', but a sight of its great and dignified buildings overbore all resistance. The sub-committee had enlisted the interest and advice of Mr Maxwell Ayrton, F.R.I.B.A., as to the suitability of the mansion and buildings for conversion into a big

[1] *See* Appendix B(2), p. 35.

school. A copy of this report, dated 17 December 1921, will be found in Appendix A and he prepared plans for the guidance of those interested. A visit to the premises at that time would have disclosed that the stuccoed columns and pillars on the north front of Stowe House, and the north front itself, needed much repair, and so did the roof; the grounds and gardens were, in the main, out of good order. Many of the small decorative buildings in the grounds were falling into decay, and some in ruins; the great avenue was largely unsightly with broken, decayed, and missing trees; the long Grecian valley, one of its beauties, was overrun by black-and-white Belgian hares; there was but one fitted bathroom in the whole mansion, and that constructed of large slate slabs, to which all water had to be carried: it was deep in the basement and had been put in during the time of the tenancy of the Comte de Paris; there was no proper water supply except such as was collected from the copper-covered roof of the beautiful oval hall, afterwards re-christened 'Assembly' — the whole place was likely to make any body of persons who inspected it shrink from the responsibility of trying to make it habitable, but Montauban and his friends did not shrink.

It was just at this time that a *Morning Post* communication stated that a careful inspection would be made before the proposal was further considered.

That was the position when the special conference of the I.A.P.S. was fixed to be held in London at the Warncliff Rooms for 28 December 1921. The Council of that body had put on its agenda for consideration the question of a new school *at Stowe*. Montauban had succeeded in interesting Dr (later Sir) Cyril Norwood, Head-master of Marlborough College, later of Harrow, and afterwards President of St John's College, Oxford, in the project, and he agreed to address the conference on the need for additional accommodation in the public schools. In the course of his address, on 28 December 1921, Dr Norwood said that there was no doubt that more parents of all classes were realizing the value of a public school education such as could be obtained in this country and in no other in the world, while more parents overseas were seeking to give their boys that great chance to improve their prospects in life. He suggested that all existing schools were then full: no great public school had been founded for sixty years; he made a detailed speech, making plain the vital need which had arisen. The conference decided unanimously that a sub-committee should pursue investigations and that a special conference should be called later.

J. F. ROXBURGH, M.A., B. ès L., FIRST HEADMASTER OF STOWE, WELCOMING
THE FIRST STOICS ON ARRIVAL ON THE OPENING DAY OF THE SCHOOL

ARRIVAL OF THE FIRST STOICS ON THE OPENING DAY OF THE SCHOOL

V

DR NORWOOD'S POSITION AS AN EXPERT ON EDUCATIONAL
topics caused his address to the conference to receive considerable
publicity in the press and aroused general interest. Just about that
time, on 31 December 1921, a report was published of a committee
appointed by the Prime Minister to inquire into the position
assigned to the classics, modern languages, literature, and history
of Ancient Greece and Rome in the educational system of the
United Kingdom, and how the proper study of them might be
maintained and in time improved. This again directed attention
towards improving our educational standards and to the accommodation and difficulties of the existing public schools.

Montauban was not without formidable opposition however —
The Times came out with a leading article against his project on
17 January 1922. Its arguments, so soon to be falsified by events,
are worth reprinting at this point.

A NEW PUBLIC SCHOOL

Though the foundation of a new public school, whether at Stowe or elsewhere,
is strictly a private affair, being the concern of private persons who are prepared
to put up the money, establish the buildings, and appoint the masters, it is not
wholly similar to that of a private school; and there are aspects, therefore, of the
Stowe proposal which are of legitimate public concern. No doubt they will be
duly weighed by the Sub-Committee of the Council of the Association of Preparatory Schools, which is charged with the consideration of the offer to that body of
the house and grounds at Stowe. In the public interest, since a public school
education is the ambition of the wealthiest and most influential portion of the
community, it would be highly deplorable if a new school at Stowe were not so
well and truly founded as to be a success, if not from the very first at least after
the first two or three years. If it is destined only to struggle for existence, it will
not provide the type of education expected from it, and will be in consequence a
waste of money and energy. If, on the other hand, it succeeds, it would be equally
regrettable if it succeeded at the expense of similar schools already in existence;
for in that case its foundation would be otiose and equally a source of unjustifiable
expense. That the expense will be high there can be no doubt, even on the

advantageous terms on which the site and the existing buildings – of whatever worth they may be for educational purposes – are to be acquired. To found anything in these days, whether it be a school or a hospital or a newspaper, costs relatively much more than it did. Two or three centuries ago a respectable foundation school could be established at comparatively small expense; a building just large enough to provide a common schoolroom and the salaries of a master or two were all that had to be ensured. Rates and taxes were unheard of; separate classrooms, playgrounds, and expensive scientific plant were neither essentials nor even luxuries. Moreover, boys could always be found; there was little or no competition among schools as there is now.

The Master of Marlborough, whose opinion is entitled to be heard, seems to have based one of his reasons for favouring the Stowe scheme on the fact that no great public school has been founded for the last sixty years or so. To this it may be replied that the prosperity of the country sixty years ago justly seemed to promise long life and success to the many new public schools then founded, whereas the country is now notoriously impoverished. It remains to be seen whether the present demand for places in the public schools will last. A year or two ago there was much more loose money in the country than there is now; and even with numbers full there are more public schools than one that find it difficult to keep things going. Fees cannot be indefinitely raised. But even if the pressure on the public schools lasts, it may be difficult for a new school to attract the best boys: their parents will prefer to send them to schools with established traditions. *Spartam nactus es* is a fine motto, but it assumes the existence even of a Sparta; and tradition is so highly esteemed in England that it is long likely to remain a predominant consideration of parents. At present it exists in a great many schools, where its advantages are capable of being extended, if only a little fresh money could be poured into them. Not all our leading public schools have occupied the position they now hold from the first; and what has been done in the past at Rugby and Shrewsbury could, were the necessary funds forthcoming, be accomplished in many other ancient, but now insufficiently endowed, schools in historic places. It seems a pity, especially at this problematic juncture in the national finances, to hazard what must in any case be a large sum of money in a new venture, if for the same sum the certainty of success can be assured in older fields.

To this extent, therefore, a real public interest lies in the proposal to turn Stowe into a public school; for money is money, wherever it is and to whomsoever it belongs, and a mistaken use of it by private persons for a laudable public purpose would be more than a private error of judgment; it would be, in a true sense, a public loss. Though the public schools are not a charge on public money, and though they can as a body well afford to contemn a good deal of the hostile criticism to which they are from time to time exposed, it will not behove their friends and supporters to embark on a venture which if it failed might seem to discredit the system. Their wiser policy would be, while the tide of popularity is exceptionally strong, to direct their influence into those channels which are already waiting to receive it.

14

Here is an answer to *The Times* leading article prepared next day, 18 January 1922, by Mrs Croom-Johnson, later, and for many years, Hon. Secretary of the Parents' Association:

To the Editor of 'The Times'

A NEW PUBLIC SCHOOL

It was with much interest, and not a little disappointment that I read your leading article yesterday. As one of the many parents who are hailing with deep satisfaction the possibility of a new foundation, it seems to me a pity that there should be even a faint suggestion from so influential an organ as *The Times* either that such a school is not needed or that the money required to establish it might be better expended on endowing further the existing foundations.

With regard to the first point, namely that at the present time there is not a sufficient demand for a NEW PUBLIC SCHOOL, I would ask the writer of the article to try this week to enter a boy aged nine years now, for any of the recognized public schools in four years time. Setting aside Eton, Harrow, and Winchester, which are well known to be full for many years to come, he would try Rugby, Clifton, Wellington, Haileybury, Marlborough, Sherborne, and many others, in vain, while the two schools offering a more modern training, Oundle and Holt, are overwhelmed with applications for admission and are unlikely to have any but chance vacancies for years.

It is true that there is less loose money in the country now than there was a year or two ago, but the parents who for the most part wish to send their sons to the public schools are just those professional people who have been impoverished ever since the war started and who, in spite of the burden of taxation and ever-increasing school fees, are wise enough to economize in everything else, rather than let their children's education suffer.

As to the second point, that money would be better employed in endowing further the historic schools, the answer is that what is most urgently needed at the moment is not extra equipment in existing schools but fresh accommodation, which will be more usefully supplied in starting a new great school than in extending others which have already grown too unwieldy and which in some cases own that they would prefer to revert to smaller numbers.

I do not share your anxiety as to a new school not attracting the best boys. Every school has had to make a beginning, and in general it is just those who are the pioneers of an educational movement who are most distinguished in after life; one may instance the many men who formed the nucleus of Clifton and of Wellington in their early days. There is one other reason why many parents are so anxious that this great scheme should go through. We want the new school to be complementary to the existing public schools rather than competitive with them. It may lack some of the things that they possess; on the other hand, there is a great chance that starting unhampered it may provide some of the things that they lack; and it is largely for this reason that the project has been greeted with so much

15

enthusiasm in private from so many different quarters. Parents (and I have talked with a great many in different parts of the country since the idea was mooted) will give the new school unhesitating and unqualified support.

The Sub-Committee of the Preparatory Schools have a very difficult task ahead of them, but they will have the good wishes of all sections of the middle classes who care about the education of their sons and who desire to extend the benefits of a good public school to numbers who are now excluded, not for any reason of incompetence or undesirability, but from sheer lack of accommodation in the existing foundations.

Yours faithfully,

RUBY E. CROOM-JOHNSON

The Parents' Association came into existence about that time, 14 February 1922, not directly connected with the shortage of public schools but intended to focus the attention of all parents on the educational position generally and to work with headmasters of public and preparatory schools on educational problems. The parents who joined that body naturally became interested, too, in the idea of a new public school. The letter in answer gives a contemporary reflection of the faith in the promoters of Stowe School and their objects.

Montauban induced a party of his parents and friends to visit Stowe House early in 1922, and once they had seen its possibilities they came out in the open as his supporters, long before the careful and full investigations which were embarked upon were completed.

VI

IT WAS NOW CONSIDERED BY MONTAUBAN AND SOME FRIENDS of his that the time had come to test the opinions of parents of possible pupils. He had obtained promises of support of the idea of a new school from a majority of about four hundred heads of preparatory schools, some, however, with reservations or criticisms. The first practical step, accordingly, was to draw up a formal proposal in print for submission to those likely to be interested, and this was done; a copy of it will be found in Appendix B(1).[1] Montauban had already delivered one or two lectures to parents of pupils at recognized preparatory schools. His next step was to give addresses to parents at a few preparatory schools in the area of the London branch.

Encouraged by what he found, Montauban decided to organize and announce the holding of a meeting of parents in March 1922 at the Hampstead Town Hall presided over by the Mayor, Alderman Frank G. Howard. The result was a large and sympathetic audience, the representative heads of a number of local preparatory schools and representative parents of intending public school boys.

It is from that date that the scheme really began to develop (a brief Press report of the meeting will be found in Appendix C). Doubts had at one time been expressed in responsible quarters whether the pressure on existing schools would continue, but after Dr Norwood's address and the Hampstead meeting that aspect of the matter disappeared.

[1] Page 34

VII

THE POSSIBILITY OF OBTAINING THE STOWE PROPERTY ITSELF and the wide body of support that the idea of the new school was now attracting, suggested that the question of raising the funds should be concentrated upon. This involved the preparation of a programme of organization, curriculum, and building. The scheme then moved a step further when it was decided, apparently by Montauban, to get together a body of persons interested in such matters. Headmasters of public schools, preparatory school masters, responsible parents, and other persons likely to be of assistance in raising finance, consented to serve, and there was formed a committee of sixteen, later called the Provisional Committee for Stowe. That Committee was set up towards the end of April 1922, and comprised the following:

CHAIRMAN

    R. P. Croom-Johnson, later K.C., M.P. (now the Hon. Mr Justice Croom-Johnson);

HEADMASTERS OF PREPARATORY SCHOOLS

    H. C. Barber (Hunstanton)
    V. S. Bryant (Maidenhead)
    C. H. Gibbs (Sloane Street)
    H. C. King (Beaconsfield), Secretary of I.A.P.S.
    E. H. Montauban (The Hall, Hampstead);

FORMER HEADMASTERS AND HEADMASTERS

    Dr A. A. David (Bishop of St Edmundsbury and Ipswich), formerly Headmaster of Rugby and Clifton
    The Rev. Frank Fletcher (Charterhouse)
    Dr Cyril Norwood (Marlborough)
    F. N. Sanderson (Oundle)
    The Rev. H. Costley White (Westminster), later Dean of Gloucester;

MEMBERS OF LEGAL PROFESSION

Sir H. Maddocks, K.C., M.P.

Stephen Miall, LL.D.

W. W. Mills;

OTHER MEMBERS

Dr George J. Jenkins, M.D.

Leslie P. Langton (of Lloyds)

Messrs Hopgood, Mills, Steele & Co., Solicitors to I.A.P.S.

Messrs Six, Smith, Ash & Co., Hon. Auditors to I.A.P.S.

Even at that time the project met serious criticism from responsible quarters entitled to respect. I print a letter in the Appendix[1] from Dr Lyttleton, Headmaster of Eton, to *The Times*, one of the most formidable of our opponents, together with Montauban's reply a few days later.[2] It is interesting, thirty years later, to read again the jeremiads. The Stowe Committee proved to be of more courageous stuff. What was their intention, and at what object were they aiming? It was to found another great public school to rank, if possible, among the first six. This was plainly put forward in a letter to the Press from the Chairman of the Committee,[3] so that the parents should be left in no doubt as to their aims and intentions.

A report from a well-known firm of architects was obtained, and the question of the availability of an ample water supply was carefully and fully investigated. The possible development of the existing buildings so as to provide all the accommodation which a modern great public school would demand was gone into in great detail, and plans were got ready for converting the great mansion to its suggested new uses.

Many other matters were to be considered, such as curriculum, size, even the question as to which code of football was to be played had to be thought about: but always was in mind the question how to find the money and how much.

---

[1] *See* Appendix D, page 41.   [2] *See* Appendix D, page 43.   [3] *See* Appendix D, page 44.

VIII

A FIRST MEETING OF THE PROVISIONAL COMMITTEE WAS held on 8 May 1922 at Mr Croom-Johnson's chambers in the Temple, and he was asked to act as chairman. Mr E. H. Montauban was appointed honorary secretary.

It was this committee which, through a smaller executive body, negotiated with the purchasers of the property at the auction sale, and which agreed provisionally on the terms of a contract. Members of it met frequently during May and June, chiefly discussing ways and means. It came very early to the conclusion that it could conceive of no purpose for which Stowe was suitable other than a public school. It prepared estimates and discussed all the necessary details of development and accommodation as the basis of opening with about one hundred pupils, and the many details before a start could be made, and how to finance it. What was to be laid down was in effect a preliminary financial programme, before an appeal could be launched for funds and for an extension in numbers term by term. It was only when all this detail work could be put forward in 'black and white' that a start could be made in approaching the preparatory schools for possible pupils and to embark upon an extension of what was called loosely enough the 'public school system' (undefined and, possibly, undefinable). A tentative scheme of education had to be laid down and a constitution for a governing body. The details to be decided were innumerable before a formal scheme could be drawn up in the shape of an appeal to all those likely to assist in the provision of financial help, either directly or in the way of promises. Finally, it was thought that a programme for the development of the school itself must be decided upon, starting with a given number of pupils and its increase, term by term, to an ultimate total number of pupils to be decided upon. The method of approach also engaged the Committee's attention, whether by public appeal or through other sources.

Although the provisional committee discussed and decided many things, the approach of the summer holidays convinced them that the problem of raising the substantial sums required to give the scheme a start (and the damaging risk of a failure was not to be contemplated as within possibilities) was too much for them in the limit of time then available, about two months. They accordingly decided to postpone their appeal until their preparations were complete and they could see their financial way more clearly. They appreciated the rising danger from the demolition squads. Possibly as the result of the publicity already achieved, most fortunately that danger attracted the attention of another committee which was engaged in proposing to start other schools for girls and boys, under the chairmanship of Lord Gisborough, and which succeeded in raising the preliminary finance required. That committee adopted the provisional Stowe scheme and ideas some time in August 1922, and during that summer they took on the whole project, set up a governing body, to which some members of the provisional committee, notably Montauban himself, were invited to join. It was that body which found and appointed J. F. Roxburgh and persuaded him to become the first headmaster, the inspiration of its first sons and the creator out of an original ninety-nine preparatory school boys of the great public school which Montauban and his early supporters had envisaged. On 12 May 1923 the school was opened for the first time. What Stowe has become, and is has been dealt with in detail elsewhere,[1] and the story of its development as a matter of buildings old and new, its playing-fields, its great educational institution, and all that that means need not be repeated here. It has been thought worth while for those who see it and its glamour today; its beautiful chapel, its grounds and playing-fields, and the glory of its long list of names of old Stoics who served their country up to death during 1939 – 1945 may be glad to have this short account of how it was first thought of and of the man who did the thinking.

[1] *Stowe: House and School*, by Alastair Macdonald. W. S. Cowell Ltd, 1951.

IX

VERY LITTLE REMAINS TO BE CHRONICLED. LORD GISBOROUGH'S Committee, having taken on the Stowe proposition and having funds available, were able to act with commendable promptitude in putting in hand the considerable building operations and making the well thought out alterations. They were quickly in a position to make a choice of the first, and, as it proved, famous Headmaster, J. F. Roxburgh. Fortunate, indeed, were they in their choice. With his help they proceeded to secure all the needed staff, teaching and otherwise, and made the selection of the first governors. Soon they were able to announce that the new school would open for the summer term and that applications for admission, limited to ninety-nine first pupils, would be considered. It is understood that the response in numbers was highly encouraging. To mark the occasion well in advance the success of the efforts of all those concerned in bringing about the new foundation was celebrated at the instance of Montauban himself, and an account of that celebration some six weeks before the opening day fitly brings our story to an end. It tells of the development of the work of the provisional committee and of the hopes of all those who met that evening to wish well to the School, then just about to start on its way.

The Times Educational Supplement, 17 March 1923 (revised)

THE NEW PUBLIC SCHOOL

OPENING OF STOWE

To celebrate the occasion of the foundation of Stowe School a dinner was given on Saturday evening, 10 March 1923, at the Hotel Central, Marylebone, by Mr and Mrs Edward Montauban. Mr Montauban is one of the Governors of Stowe, a prominent member of the Preparatory Schoolmasters' Association, and a leading figure among those who conceived the idea of establishing a new public school in the historic mansion near Buckingham. About ninety guests were present to meet Lord Gisborough, Chairman of the Governing Body, Lady Gisborough, and the Headmaster, Mr J. F. Roxburgh.

Mr Montauban, proposing the toast 'Coadjutores nostri', said that many people had felt three or four years ago that there was a need for wider opportunities of education for boys in England, and some two and a half years ago a voice was raised to try if that need could not be met. Presently two or three answered the call, and then three or four more, and gradually the cause and the band of workmen grew until finally a good start had been made. These were men of vision and of imagination – men of large heart – and when he said 'men' he included most emphatically women also. A critical time came last summer, when, in spite of all that the provisional committee could do, under their most energetic and capable chairman, Mr Croom-Johnson, they had to confess themselves done, at any rate for the moment. They had simply to lie low and wait, and trust that deliverance might fall from the heavens. At a point when the auction of Stowe was going to take place in ten days time, and when in all probability the place would be sold to the housebreaker, deliverance dropped almost from the skies. Lord Gisborough with his helpers came to the rescue, and their power, their influence, their enterprise, and their courage saved the situation. Had it not been for what they did Stowe would have been by now in all probability a derelict instead of a pride, glory, and hope for generations to come.

Mr R. P. Croom-Johnson: I am here to ask you to drink the health of our host and of his wife, Mr and Mrs Montauban. I have really no right to butt in on this occasion, although I have been described as one of the persons who helped in the foundation of this very considerable enterprise; but I am not worthy to be called an apostle, and anything I did I did merely on the direct inspiration of our good friend Montauban. I did so because that great driving force of his, animating his own great ideals about Stowe and the necessity for a new public school in England, urged him forward and compelled me and others to join him in trying to attain his ambition. We could not hold a candle to him, with his clear foresight, and nothing so far has been said about the great part he took. Two or three years ago he was ploughing a lonely furrow, but the little candle which Montauban then lighted has at least started a great conflagration in the world of education in Modern England.

The educationalists have known Montauban as a man who has been pressing forward this idea of his for a long time. I am certain that every one of you parents and others with whom he has discussed this matter will have realized that he had ideals which were sustaining him, and that he had at heart the best interests of the education of the youth of our country.

The reason that Stowe exists is that Montauban started the idea. It is he whose imagination was touched by the notion not only of founding a great new school but also of founding it at Stowe.

ORIGIN OF THE SCHEME

Lord Gisborough disclaimed any responsibility for starting the Stowe scheme. It was Mr Montauban who conceived the idea. 'A great many years ago I was persuaded to become a Governor of Uppingham, and finally I had the pleasure of taking part in the appointment of a gentleman who is present tonight, the

Rev. Henry Mackenzie, as headmaster of that school. He did enormous service in the only too short time that he was there. That has nothing to do with this case, but eventually I was forced against my will to take the chair at another school, and then from that came this movement. In the meantime most of us realized that there was a great need for another first-class public school. Stowe had been selected and had been favourably reported upon, and the only thing wanted was finance. I want you to realize that someone with greater power and influence was there to find the money and induce people to lend their aid to this new school; but by a chain of accidents I have to champion it tonight.'

In considering any such venture as this, he continued, there were always bound to be some pessimists, and he had heard men of high degree say it was bound to be a failure. They said that what was wanted was not to add a new school but to enlarge the schools that already existed. Lord Gisborough said he had always thought that even Eton would be much better if the number of boys that composed it were considerably less, and this applied to other very large schools. There came a limit to the number that one man could really look after. Some people said there might be a demand for more schools today, on account of a large number of people having made money during the war and being in a position to educate their children, but that this demand would soon die down. Yet surely enlarging an old school meant building more houses, and if ultimately numbers decreased, these houses would not be needed. He thought it time to start a new school on modern lines, and it was for that reason that he had taken part in starting this one at Stowe. The pessimists who asserted that it could not be done were wrong, because it had been done. The school was there, and they had sufficient funds to start it. They had on their register the names of more boys than they could take. Something like five hundred were wanting to come, but they would be able to house only something like ninety boys at the start in May, and only about another hundred for the following term. With future entries they would have more than the present buildings would hold, and would have to appeal to the public for an endowment fund to build masters' houses, where a larger number could be stowed away. [*Laughter and cheers.*] In the meantime, they had a really tip-top headmaster. He believed that Mr Roxburgh had the courage and all the gifts of mind to fulfil an extremely difficult task.

Stowe House, with its great historical traditions, would in itself make a tradition for the boys and arouse in them a spirit which they would carry out into the world. Although quite satisfied as to the financial aspect, the Governors would like to have the interest and sympathy of all who had the cause of higher education at heart. They could help outside the school itself by destroying the pessimism of those who opposed it. They could also help the endowment fund, so that Stowe might not remain a small school. There were many ways in which help could be given apart from money. In the magnificent library the book-shelves were empty; would some kind friends come along and help to fill these shelves and help train the young boy to read history and all that was best in literature? The name of the school would be 'Stowe School', and for short 'Stowe'.

Mr Roxburgh, the Headmaster, responding to the toast of 'Stowe School', said that he was reading Percival's Life the other day, and read there that he made Clifton into a little Rugby, and he understood that something of the same kind was done at the foundation of Haileybury. He himself was a Carthusian, and a loyal one, and had been for many years at another public school. But Stowe was not going to be a little Charterhouse or a little Lancing; it was going to be a little Stowe, and very shortly it was going to be a big Stowe. They had already entries for every term but two till 1934. They were not going to do only what the other schools had done, but they were going to use what they had done as the basis, and they were not going to do anything odd or at random. They possessed 144 letters written to the first founders of Stowe by preparatory school-masters—men of wide experience. Their views were of the greatest possible value, and the school had a first-class asset not only in those letters but in the men who wrote them. It would be presumptuous and foolish to suggest that Stowe was going to do at once what older schools had not done, but if in the fullness of time and in abler hands than his own, Stowe did not make a contribution of its own to English education, the venture would not have been justified. No one could be absolutely contented with public school education as it was. Had we learnt to preserve the freshness, the eagerness, the curiosity, the unclipped imagination of childhood, such as they were when the boys were sent to school? And, secondly, had we learnt how to harness and use for good all those new powers which were released in a boy at the budding of his manhood? All public school masters of the old schools, as well as of the new, must admit that those problems still awaited solution.

He was standing within a few feet of the Headmaster of Charterhouse and of the Headmaster of Westminster, and would tell them straight out that they would never beat Stowe at football, unless they changed to Rugby. He had secured a man to start the cricket who was believed to be one of the finest coaches in England. With regard to work, no one would suspect a new school of being about to neglect science. They had already at Stowe a first-class biological laboratory in the five hundred acres of beautiful English wood and lake and park. In languages they hoped to do well, and there was one language in which he was particularly interested – the English language itself. Sir Henry Newbolt's Committee pointed out in their report that the culture of France was not better than that of England, but more diffused. It was based upon the French language, and that state of affairs could be reproduced in England. There were two other languages which exercised the parental heart – Latin and Greek. There were some boys who could get no good out of even elementary Latin; others who could get good out of elementary Latin but not out of advanced Latin. For both classes they would make provision, and they would also provide Greek for those who deserved it. For most boys he firmly believed that there was no more potent instrument for teaching clear thought and clear expression than the early stages of the Latin language. But in his own teaching career he had come to form two conclusions: the first was that in the education of a boy the person who played the most important part was the boy himself. The second was that if one wanted to educate a boy one must find out something that he liked to do and did well, and get him to do it as long as he could and as hard as he could. Boys for the most part educated themselves, and in the athletic and corporate life of a great school there was a man-making machinery which, on the moral and physical sides, was unequalled in the world. But, none the less, the trainers of the mind had a work to do: teaching had its part to play, if teaching were interpreted as helping and encouraging to learn. And that part was twofold. They had to teach boys scientific subjects, that they might take their share in controlling Nature and exploring Nature – the age-long tasks of the race – and, on another plane, that they might know fact from fable and gain an eager and fearless love of knowledge. And they had to teach them literary subjects, that they might gain the power of clear thought and clear expression, a quickened imagination, and a swift and catholic gift of sympathy. 'There is one thing more that we can teach boys at Stowe – or one more thing that we can let them learn. You will know what I mean if you have ever looked up one of our long green valleys at the great south front of Stowe in the soft light of a spring day. Perhaps you stood where you could see the lake too, and near by where the wood comes forward into the green; you may have had a glimpse of an Ionic column or the corner of a Doric frieze, just catching a glint of sunlight, like a shy nymph among the branches: and at the back of all the great pillared house itself. If you have such memories as that of Stowe, you will know what I mean when I say that if we do not fail wholly in our purpose, every boy who goes out from Stowe will know beauty when he sees it all the rest of his life.' The motto of the school will be 'Praesto et Persto'.

The dinner was preceded by the following grace: 'Benedic, Domine, nobis et scholae nostrae Stovensi quam ad majorem tuam gloriam curamus constituendam, Qui vivis et regnas et es Deus in saecula saeculorum'.

X

FINALLY, AS A MEMORIAL OF MONTAUBAN'S PART IN ALL this, many of his friends decided to put on record in the School Library what he had done. It took this form. His original Hampstead scholars' parents (after the suggestion at his dinner from Lord Gisborough about the empty shelves in the great library), through a small committee of four, provided by subscription a collection of standard books to form a complete English section of the library of some hundreds of volumes as a gift to Montauban in recognition of his work. Great care was taken to buy only volumes printed in beautiful and plain type, well bound. A special book-plate in each volume said this:

Presented for the use of the Library
by

to Edward Henry Montauban, M.A.,
who first imagined a School at Stowe
and became a member of its original
Governing Body

On 18 July 1923 Montauban received this testimonial at a meeting of 'parents', and on the next day he handed it over to the Headmaster with a letter in the following words:

My Dear Headmaster,

Most kind and generous action on the part of a number of parents of my boys has placed me in a position to ask the acceptance by Stowe School of a collection of books for the School Library.

These have been specially selected and will be delivered to you tomorrow. I shall be indeed proud and happy if they may be retained and used by the boys and the masters as you shall find convenient.

If this gift may be taken as a small token of my interest in and zeal for Stowe School, I shall be more than gratified.

Yours very sincerely,

(*Signed*) E. H. MONTAUBAN

SOME OF THE EARLIEST STOICS INSPECTING THE SOUTH FRONT ON THE OPENING
DAY AFTER ARRIVAL

EDWARD HENRY MONTAUBAN, THE INSPIRATION
OF THE STOWE IDEAL, WATCHING THE FIRST
STOICS ARRIVING ON THE OPENING DAY

The volumes appeared in the English Section of the Library marked with a suitable brass plate, 'Montauban Presentation'.

They have been well used and have made an appeal to the Stoics, for whom they were originally intended, as a recent visit to the section of the Library plainly showed.

R.P.C.-J.

STOWE

REPORT BY MAXWELL AYRTON, Esq., f.r.i.b.a.,
DATED 17 DECEMBER 1921
To: E. H. MONTAUBAN, Esq., m.a.

Dear Sir,

Following our conference on 27 November and our subsequent visit to Stowe on 3 December with Mr Sydney How and Mr A. T. Bean, I beg to report as follows:

SITUATION. Stowe is situated about three miles from Buckingham, a typical old English town.

The estate lies on high ground to the north-west of the town, 450 feet above the sea level, and is entered through a triumphal archway at the end of a wide avenue one and a half miles in length. From this point there is a vista across the valley and lake to the south front of the House, about three-quarters of a mile away. The house is approached by a winding road past the lake to the forecourt and entrance on the north side. The park itself is 282 acres in extent, and is one of the most magnificent in the kingdom. It was here that 'Capability' Brown was born and bred, first a gardener's boy and finally head gardener to Lord Cobham, developing his love of landscape gardening from the park as we now see it — a great achievement of forestry and landscape gardening upon a colossal scale. It needs little imagination to conjure up the possibilities of such a place as the work and playground of a community of boys.

The house, designed by Vanbrugh about 1707 and altered and added to by Kent and others all famous in their day, is conceived upon a scale of grandeur needing such surroundings. The harmony of the grounds with the house and the perfect placing of the latter prevents the feeling of discomfort one might otherwise have in approaching a house of such dimensions – it appears perfectly right and proper in its setting, no undue display, merely the outward assurance that upon entering one will be surrounded by the memories of a great past.

The house has been very little touched during the last hundred years, and room after room offers varying examples of decorative art of great interest and, in many cases, delight. The accompanying plans have been prepared for this report and must not be taken as complete surveys of the building but merely as diagrams giving the accommodation, size of rooms, etc, approximately.

The house is planned upon lines frequently adopted at the period in which it was built, a central block comprising the great reception and state rooms, with side wings accommodating the private and living rooms. The so-called ground floor is reached by a great flight of steps up to the main entrance to the hall and state rooms, and below this floor at the ground level is the floor containing all the kitchen and service offices as well as the chapel and library and a series of sitting rooms with windows to the south or garden front.

The buildings would lend themselves to adaptation for school purposes. Where a building has been well planned originally it may always be converted and rearranged satisfactorily, and in this instance the planning of the house is of a high standard for its period, the services to the various rooms being particularly well arranged. There is space for the accommodation of a school of, say, 150 boys and staff, including all dormitories, living rooms, form rooms and laboratories, etc, in the existing buildings. Subsequently, as numbers increased and funds became available, it would be necessary to build separate form rooms and laboratory blocks, maintaining the existing buildings chiefly as the communal and administrative centre.

PROCEDURE. Should the scheme be proceeded with, I suggest the method employed should be as follows:

(a) To prepare a complete and accurate survey of the entire buildings, including all sewage and surface water drains, water, gas, and other services, together with detailed reports upon their condition and upon the grounds and park.

(*b*) To form a small committee to draw up a schedule, so far as may be possible, of what will be the ultimate total accommodation and requirements of the proposed school.

(*c*) The same committee to draw up a similar schedule for the commencement of the school with, say, 50 to 100 boys.

(*d*) To prepare plans for the complete scheme. These plans need not be in detail but should give the general lines to be adhered to in years to come as the school develops, in order that no step in this direction may subsequently be found to interfere with the economical and natural growth of the school.

(*e*) To prepare plans in detail of the work essential to be done before the school may be started.

CONDITION OF EXISTING BUILDINGS: EXTERNAL. The whole of the buildings are of brick faced with stucco, some of the cornices and architectural ornaments being built up of timber and oak laths finished with stucco. Throughout the stucco is in a bad state of repair, having been allowed to fall into decay with little or no attempt to repair it for many years. Stucco is a form of protective facing that requires constant care, as it deteriorates at a rapidly increasing rate if neglected. The woodwork generally does not appear to have suffered severely and the roofs are, generally speaking, sound and in good repair. The garden buildings and outbuildings have suffered most and in some cases are derelict.

INTERNAL. Internally the conditions of repair are remarkably good, and this may be ascribed very largely to the care given by Mr North, who has been employed upon the estate for the last fifty years. The cooking apparatus and fittings to the kitchens and offices are antiquated and useless for present-day conditions. This also applies to the sanitary arrangements throughout the house. There is not a single bath and the water-closets which were put in many years ago do not meet modern requirements, either in their situations or fittings.

WATER. Attached is Mr A. T. Bean's report upon the water supply.

REPAIRS, ETC. Apart from any structural alterations, it would not be possible to prepare any specification of dilapidations upon which satisfactory or economical tenders could be obtained. Any contractor being invited to give an inclusive lump-sum estimate for such work would be compelled to give an outside figure to cover his risks. I am therefore of the opinion that the sound and economical way of dealing with the question of repairs and subsequent alterations and additions would be to set up at the start a small building department of all trades under the control of a thoroughly competent resident clerk of works. By this means the works could be carried out gradually, as and where most needed and at actual working cost. The success of such a department depends very largely upon the man in control, and a man should be chosen who would undertake the position as a permanent one. Each individual of the staff of such a department should also be selected so far as possible with the same point in view, for the fostering of teamwork and the pride taken in it is the surest way to good and economical building.

CONCLUSION. The initial cost of repair and subsequent upkeep both of grounds and buildings preclude the possibility of carrying out the scheme without the aid of a large endowment. If such endowment can be found, there is no doubt in my mind that this historic house and park must have a great and increasing effect in creating a fine tradition among those who spend their lives in it.

The scheme is one of high ideal, and it is only as such that the acceptance of STOWE as the nucleus of the foundation of a new public school should be considered.

I am, dear Sir,

Your obedient servant,

(*Signed*) MAXWELL AYRTON.

Leaflet which Preparatory School Headmasters might kindly distribute amongst Parents

THE PROPOSED NEW PUBLIC SCHOOL

A number of preparatory school headmasters have had under consideration a project to found one more great public school.

A site and buildings have been offered as a gift, subject to a time limit and the raising of a proper endowment fund.

It is earnestly hoped that this project may materialize and that it may be possible to open the school for a start in September next.

Those in charge of the scheme have decided on certain necessary but reasonable restrictions as regards admissions, in particular it is required that every boy should have been *recommended* and *nominated* by his preparatory school headmaster.

They venture to commend to parents the following suggestions:

That parents, old boys, and friends of individual preparatory schools be invited to make donations (not recurring subscriptions) towards the 'Nomination Fund' of their chosen preparatory school. This fund should be administered by the headmaster of that school in obtaining and holding *for that school* 'Nominations' or 'Exhibitions' for entry. Each £50 contained in that fund would obtain for that preparatory school one 'Nomination Right', or £150 would obtain an 'Exhibition Right'.

The constitution of the foundation admits of altogether 400 of the former and 100 of the latter; individual preparatory schools will not be limited as to the number of 'RIGHTS' to be held so long as there remain any available.

They believe, in view of the difficulty of securing a guaranteed vacancy in the existing great public schools, the plan here suggested may be welcomed and supported by many parents as a means whereby they may benefit themselves, their boys, and the preparatory school in which they are interested.

Signed, for the Sub-Committee,

11 Belsize Avenue Hampstead London, N.W.3

E. H. MONTAUBAN, M.A.

Appendix B (2)

To *the Members of the Association of Preparatory Schools*

THE PROPOSED NEW PUBLIC SCHOOL

Dear Sir,

This subject came before the general Conference last December, and it was unanimously decided that the Sub-Committee should pursue investigations and that a Special Conference should be called later.

The Sub-Committee has now reported to the Council, and it is hoped that the Conference will be held within the next two months.

It is only right that I should let you be aware that some members of the Council consider that the matter is outside our province *as an Association*, they fear that by taking action we should lay ourselves open to the criticism 'that it is not our business to run a public school'. May I suggest that the proposition is not that we should in any way *run* a public school but merely that we should give the lead in *starting* one. To do this is, I maintain, our business, seeing that the thing is wanted and that nobody else will undertake the initial step.

Some of the suggestions and conclusions of the Sub-Committee are given below for your information, and I would ask your consideration of them and then the very great courtesy of a reply, long or short, stating your opinion; this, whichever way it tended, would be of very great value to the Sub-Committee. The fact is, an enormous amount of work is entailed in the promulgation of this scheme – it has to be presented ultimately to the whole British public – it is therefore absolutely essential to the conduct of our endeavour that we should have ascertained the opinions and probable actions of all the preparatory headmasters.

'The Sub-Committee and others have inspected the grounds and buildings at Stowe, which have been offered, subject to a time limit

35

of two months, and to a proper endowment being forthcoming, and they are of the opinion that these could be made to serve admirably. Up to about 200 boys could be accommodated in the existing buildings without formidable alterations. Some £35,000 might be required to adapt and equip for this number; under favourable conditions a small start might be made in September.

'The following are some special points:

(1) The Foundation should contain nothing of the nature of a private, a sectarian, or a fad school, but it should be constituted by Deed, held by Trustees, and controlled by Governors in the public interest.

(2) The curriculum, general activities and special features should be decided by a committee appointed for the purpose.

(3) The fees should be fixed, provisionally, at £150 per annum.

(4) Special consideration should be devoted to the regulations governing the choice of boys for admission; one very special requirement being the personal recommendation and definite "Nomination" of a boy by his preparatory headmaster. This proviso, as will be seen at once, would benefit Stowe, for it would guarantee the worth of candidates and would eliminate the possible aspersion that the new school was but the refuge of rotters, rejects, or the superannuated; at the same time it would benefit the preparatory master in giving him the certain call on one, two, or more places at Stowe, according to the number of "Rights" which his school might hold.

'The "Rights" would be limited to 400 "Options" and 100 "Exhibitions".

'For each contribution of £50 a preparatory school would become the holder of one "Option". This confers the call, at ordinary fees, on one place permanently at Stowe.

'For each contribution of £150 a preparatory school would become the holder of one "Exhibition". This confers the call, at £20 reduction, on one place permanently at Stowe.

'Several such "Options" or "Exhibitions" could be acquired and held by any preparatory school.'

36

The Sub-Committee go on to say that in view of the fact that all the above 'Rights' are to be held and exercised by preparatory schools, it is hoped that very many headmasters will interest themselves in raising contributions with which to purchase or subscribe for these 'Rights' for their own schools.

In case there are some headmasters who dislike the idea of themselves making an appeal, the Sub-Committee have prepared a quantity of leaflets (specimen enclosed) which might perhaps be used for the purpose; copies of these may be obtained by return of post by any who will write to me for them.

In conclusion, may I ask your most kind indulgence should this letter appear to you as a liberty on my part. I do not mean to be officious or presumptuous, and am only venturing to act as the mouthpiece of the many men who really feel that something ought to be done to provide the further facilities which our boys do need when they leave our preparatory schools.

Yours faithfully,

E. H. MONTAUBAN.

11 Belsize Avenue
Hampstead
London, N.W.3

Appendix C

REPORT OF PUBLIC MEETING AT HAMPSTEAD, MARCH 1922

PROPOSED NEW PUBLIC SCHOOL AT BUCKINGHAM

(Extracted from 'Hampstead & St John's Wood Advertiser', 16 March 1922)

That the scheme for a new public school appeals to parents and residents in Hampstead, and that there is a felt and insistent need for such a school were clearly evidenced at the largely attended meeting held at the Town Hall, Hampstead, on Tuesday last week.

The Mayor of Hampstead presided, and he was supported by the principals of many of the Hampstead preparatory schools and the Rev. A. Jackson (Vicar of St Paul's, Avenue Road).

The Chairman said the question of education had been brought prominently forward through the 'Geddes & Co.'s Cuts'. All would agree that they desired reduced income tax and rates, but did not desire economy at the expense of education. Greater educational facility was needed among those who were anxious to pay for their sons' education, but the great public schools were full up and would be for some years, and it was difficult for boys, unless they possessed great intellectual ability or private influence, to obtain entrance into public schools.

Mr E. H. Montauban, who is the moving spirit in the project, said he appreciated the public-spirited way the audience had come forward, and congratulated them upon accepting the opportunity and privilege of being among the original founders of the new great public school of England, for whether or no the scheme materialized then or later was beside the question, the idea was sound and would prevail. He first dealt with the need of founding another great public school, owing to the congested state existing in the public schools, and the insistent demand from parents for a modified curriculum in public schools. The public school type of training essentially appealed to the English character, and he briefly enumerated other causes – the preparatory schools, which had enormously increased, themselves acting as tributaries to the public schools – which had resulted not only in crowding out the accommodation but had produced long waiting-lists. By means of lantern slides he illustrated the grandeur of Stowe and the beauty of its grounds, and urged the suitability of the place and the greatness of the opportunity for founding there a new great public school. An offer had been made of the mansion and the grounds (some 280 acres) for this purpose, subject to a time limit, and the raising of a proper endowment. The sum of £200,000 was required, an amount, he realized, impossible to raise except by the wide organization and earnest co-operation of parents throughout the country, and by the aid of personal munificence. He felt that the help of the philanthropist could hardly be expected till some exhibition of earnestness had been shown by the parents, and he proposed that this should be evidenced by the response which they could make to the scheme which he suggested for the start. This scheme proposed that the various preparatory schools throughout the country should interest their respective groups of parents, and invite from them contributions which would enable the preparatory schools severally to purchase one, two or more 'Rights' conferring the privilege of nominating pupils to the new school. A total of 500 places ultimately was to be aimed at, and 500 Rights created, the purchase money of these would be sufficient for the equipment and the alterations necessary for the start. Further funds might be raised at low interest or by debentures. If only such promises of support could be secured, this would be an evidence of sincerity which might attract the substantial aid of wealthy men towards the necessary permanent endowment. Success had been achieved in the past when Clifton, Cheltenham, Marlborough, Wellington, and many others were first started, and they had far fewer advantages than are now being offered.

Mr R. P. Croom-Johnson put the case from the point of view of a parent with three sons who needed, firstly, to be sure of a public school for them as they reached the proper age and, secondly, a school whose curriculum and arrangements should be designed for present-day requirements. In an earnest and effective speech he urged the necessity, and pleaded for the support of his hearers. He said that he wanted 499 men to back up the offer of £50, which on the spot he was proud to make as the first contributor to this great national work.

Questions from the audience were put by Dr Miall, who wished to secure second place in the list for his donation, and by various others.

Dr A. R. Roche, in a few telling phrases, expressed his belief in the scheme and proposed as a resolution 'That this meeting of parents and residents in Hampstead considers that a pressing public need would be served by the establishment at Stowe of one more great public school with a curriculum to meet the wants of the present day'.

This was seconded by Mr J. G. Granville Grenfell, and carried unanimously.

THE NEW PUBLIC SCHOOL

DR E. LYTTELTON'S LETTER TO 'THE TIMES', 29 APRIL 1922

To the Editor of 'The Times'

Sir,

May I utter a word of caution to those who are being invited to subscribe largely to the costly and attractive project of equipping and starting a new public school?

We hear a good deal of the present congestion of all sorts of schools, due, I suppose, to many boys and girls being kept at school longer than formerly. But can anyone reckon on this congestion continuing? For if it does not, the expenditure, at this time, of many thousands — most of which will be drawn from other charities — will be a flagitious waste.

But worse than a waste, it will deal a serious injury to many public schools, day schools, grammar schools, etc, in the following way: Supposing — what is far from improbable — the financial stress continues, and the already large number of parents who are driven to day schools, cheap private schools, or elementary schools grows larger, by the time the grand new venture is started it will mean that there will be at least one big school too many.

The effect of that is that several other schools of a similar character will be depleted of pupils, till they work at a loss; and the result is, of course, less efficiency, prolonged anxiety, failure among the boys of belief in their respective schools (a most serious matter), and waste of staff, equipment, premises, etc, etc.

In short, to start a new school in times like these is wholly unjustifiable, unless the need for it can be clearly demonstrated. Instead of which, headmasters tell me they expect the congestion to come to an end at any moment. If this happens, it will not be due, as the promoters of the new school assume, to lack of places, but simply to shrunken incomes.

Of course, if another Christ's Hospital could be founded, the problem of parents' poverty would be greatly mitigated. But, I gather, the new venture is not to be of this kind at all. It is to be an ordinary public school, with the usual number of scholarships, bursaries, etc, if funds permit. But hitherto many of these benefactions have not helped poverty so much as they have advertised success in examinations.

Nor, again, is there any guarantee that the new school will be more adapted to modern requirements than the old one. In so far as the latter fail in this respect, it is because there is no agreement in any quarter as to what those requirements are. Doubtless fresh experiments ought to be tried; but that is exactly what has been going on for the last seventy years; so that in curriculum, in methods, in equipment, and in spirit — in short, in every respect — our boarding schools have been revolutionized.

But should this view of the situation prove to be erroneous, and should the congestion continue, the right way to deal with it would be for a board to be formed of half a dozen patriots who understand education — if there are as many — to ask the public for £100,000 for the subsidizing of existing institutions, especially the cathedral schools. This would be for a gradual extension of their premises, or for the meeting of the needs of poverty by increased benefactions.

One of the promoters of the new scheme tells me the only argument against this suggestion is that it would not 'catch the popular imagination' so well as the more dazzling re-creation of the Stowe mansion. I am afraid he is right. But if the public are afraid of my suggestion, they ought to be far more afraid of his.

Yours faithfully,

E. LYTTELTON.

Overstrand, Norfolk
April 26.

To the Editor of 'The Times'

Sir,

The tenor of Dr Lyttleton's letter in your issue of 29 April may be found in the words which he uses in his opening and his closing lines – the words 'caution' and 'afraid'. His argument appears to be built on the assumption that the country is going down into bankruptcy, and he counsels us to wait until we are prosperous before we make provision for that prosperity.

I would ask, is this the spirit in which to set about achieving prosperity? Is this an ideal way for the upbringing of our boys? Can we expect to turn out men of enterprise and courage if the schools of England are to be afraid of a new competitor, and if no new venture is to be attempted unless success is guaranteed beforehand?

But the fact that five of our great headmasters are on our 'Provisional Committee for Stowe' is proof that this is not the spirit of the existing public schools, and the fact that already we have received letters from all over the country urging us to continue in our efforts, gives assurance of the real need.

Dr Lyttelton's letter will have helped our cause if only it has emphasized the fact that to persevere in face of criticism from such a distinguished quarter needs courage, and that to support the scheme while its fate is yet in the balance would be the act of a patriot and a man of vision.

Here is a chance for the philanthropist to give his help and see in his lifetime the growth and fruit of his good deed. Our committee is to hold its first meeting on Monday, 8 May. I would dearly like to have received by then a sheaf of letters with promises of support which I could lay before the members then.

Yours faithfully,

11 Belsize Avenue
Hampstead
London, N.W.3

E. H. MONTAUBAN,
Hon. Secretary, the Provisional
Committee for Stowe

LETTER FROM THE CHAIRMAN OF THE PROVISIONAL COMMITTEE FOR STOWE TO THE 'SUNDAY TIMES'

To the Editor of the 'Sunday Times'

PALACE OF STOWE PROJECT

In his 'Public Schools' column in the *Sunday Times* last week Mr A. Podmore commented on the new public school which it is proposed to inaugurate at the mansion of Stowe, which, together with its grounds of some 280 acres, it is hoped to acquire for the purpose. Mr Podmore also voiced the query whether the new school would start on Rugger or Soccer, a query answered by Mr R. P. Croom-Johnson, of 1 Hare Court, Temple, E.C., who informs us that he is given to understand that the Rugby code will be followed.

But, says Mr Croom-Johnson, before this stage is reached there is the necessity of finding the funds, and it is on this topic that I venture to write to you.

The promoters of the scheme, continues Mr Croom-Johnson, have decided in favour of the modern curriculum for which so many parents are in search; but this does not mean, as your correspondents seem to imagine, that the idea of a modern curriculum necessarily connotes the wholesale exclusion of classical learning or tradition – far from it. Nor does it mean the division of the school into 'sides'.

It does, however, mean, as I understand it, greater attention being paid to the literature, history, and development of our own land, with classics taking their own true position with modern languages, science, and the like, as part of an attempt at an introduction to the general field of learning. Specialization should start not earlier than the age of sixteen, leaving the University to complete the work on the chosen branch.

Education on some such lines as these has proved to be not merely what modern parents want, but mightily beneficial to the pupils at Oundle and also at Holt. The intention is now to found another great public school for 500 boys to rank, if possible, among the first six at a time when the demand for all public schools is very far in excess of the places available. The wonderful buildings have been promised by a munificent benefactor, subject to a proper endowment fund of £200,000 being raised.

In addition, about £35,000 for equipment is required, and this latter amount is to be raised in the main by the purchase of nomination rights of £50 each available through recognized preparatory schools. As a parent, I believe in the modern curriculum, and I have been privileged to become the first to promise a Stowe 'right'. I have no other interest in the matter, and no other claim on your readers' attention; merely as a parent I ask 499 other parents to join with me. Further information can be obtained from Mr E. H. Montauban, M.A., of 11 Belsize Avenue, Hampstead, on behalf of the preparatory schools which are 'behind' the movement.

STOWE SCHOOL

House List, Summer Term, 1923

TEMPLE HOUSE

(MR. I. M. CROSS)

Name	*School No.*	*Name*	*School No.*
Croft, A.	110	Henry, R. L.	220
		Izat, A.	250
Bowie, A. G.	56	Jackson, H. B. B.	255
Robinson, H. E.	416	Jones, L. C.	266
		Kemp-Gee, E. A.	279
Avory, E. R.	20	Luddington, W. H. C.	298
Barlow, C. M.	30	Marshall, J. R.	303
Begbie, C. W. H.	43	Martens, J.	305
Bertram, O. H. J.	45	Middleton, J. H.	322
Bowen, C. A. C.	54	Montagu-Scott ma., M. S.	331
Bramley, D. S.	60	Montagu-Scott mi., D. S.	332
Buckley, G. M.	67	Mowbray, B. C. H.	336
Cook, A. G. A.	96	Nixon, J. C.	355
Corbett, G.	99	Oxley, W. N. C.	373
Cowell, A. M.	100	Pocock, S. F. H.	390
Cox, E. R.	103	Richards, E.	408
Craster, W. G. S.	106	Rivers-Moore, L. G.	412
Creed, C. S.	108	Rogers, S. C.	421
Crookston, C. M.	115	Rowse, G. E.	428
Curtis, R. W.	120	Sanderson, J. C.	435
Daw, L. A.	128	Sansome, P.	438
Dawson, J. E.	130	Searle, D. H. I.	450
Day, B. W.	132	Smallman, J. S.	460
Falconer, P. M.	165	Strauss, L. E.	472
Franklin, P. J.	170	Tickler, C. A.	495
Ginn, B. D. S.	180	Turrall, H. D.	515
Griffin, G. A.	190	Walker, R. L.	541
Harriss, B. S.	205	Webb, S. E.	551
Healey, A. C.	215		

STOWE SCHOOL

House List, Summer Term, 1923

BRUCE HOUSE

(THE REV. ERNEST EARLE)

Name	School No.	Name	School No.
Wilson, D. F.	1	Holmes, R. W. L.	240
		Jessop, H. R.	260
Butler, The Hon. G. C. S. P.	70	Jones, C. B.	265
		Kish, E.	281
Andrews, R. A.	10	Langley, C. M.	288
Beard, R. W.	40	Lord, M. E. C.	293
Blackburn, T. K.	50	Mayhew, J. de P. G.	208
Bookless, J. R. M.	53	McCallin, S. G.	312
Boyd-Carpenter, J. A.	58	McLean, J.	317
Campbell, G. A.	80	Miller, V. K.	325
Cochrane, O. K.	94	Murdoch, R. M.	341
Cowell, C. P.	101	Pearson, C. J. P.	385
Culverwell, R. D.	118	Robinson, A. R. W.	415
Davie, P. H. W.	126	Rogers, A. P. C.	420
Dean, H.	134	Savill, P. S.	441
Denny, A. M. C.	136	Scott, K. L.	445
Drayson, F. H.	138	Silcock, W. R. K.	455
Dunlop, W. W.	140	Sinclair, A.	465
Dunsford ma., D. A.	142	Swan, S. C.	477
Dunsford mi., A.	143	Walker, R. H. C.	540
Hartland-Swann ma., J. J.	210	Webb, C. B.	550
Hartland-Swann mi., C. H.	211	Wight-Boycott, A. H.	560
Heyworth, H.	225	Yorke, P. R.	590